BEYOND DINOSAURS! My First Book About FLYING CREATURES

Interior and Cover Designer: Gabe Nansen
Art Producer: Janice Ackerman
Annie Choi, Editor and Maxine Marshall, Associate Editor
Illustrations: © 2020 Annalisa and Marina Durante
Author Photo: © 2020 Jack Wilson
Illustrators Photo: © 2020 Fredi Marcarini

ISBN: Print 978-1-64611-934-9 | eBook 978-1-64739-284-0

R0

BEYOND DINOSAURS! My First Book About FLYING CREATURES

By Cary Woodruff

Illustrations by Annalisa & Marina Durante

ROCKRIDGE PRESS

ALL ABOUT PREHISTORIC FLIGHT!

A very long time ago, many strange animals lived on Earth, including flying **prehistoric** creatures.

We learn everything that we know about dinosaurs and other prehistoric creatures from **fossils**. **Paleontologists** are the scientists who dig up and study the fossils of prehistoric life. Thanks to fossils, we know which prehistoric animals could fly, what they ate, and how long ago they lived.

Only some prehistoric flying creatures were dinosaurs. Birds **evolved** from small, meat-eating dinosaurs and survive to this day. Other creatures, like the **pterosaurs (TER-a-SORS)**, flew above the heads of early dinosaurs.

Pterosaurs were flying reptiles that lived at the same time as dinosaurs. Although they looked like dinosaurs, they belonged to a different family.

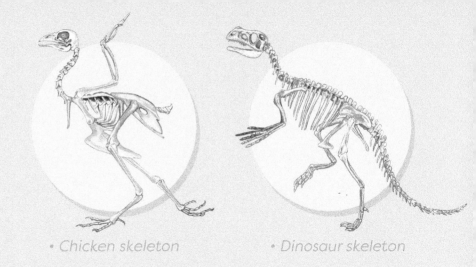

A hummingbird, ostrich, pigeon, eagle, penguin, peacock, chicken—every single bird you know is a living dinosaur!

• Chicken skeleton • Dinosaur skeleton

Paleontologists know that dinosaurs and pterosaurs are different because all dinosaurs have a big hole in their hip socket and a large **crest** on their upper arm bone, and pterosaurs don't.

We know a lot about these flying prehistoric creatures, but because of new discoveries, what we know is always changing. Maybe one day you will help make a new discovery!

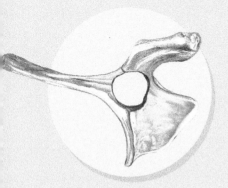
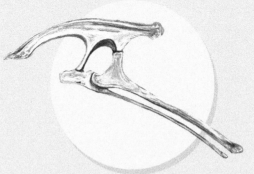

On the dinosaur family tree, dinosaurs and pterosaurs are like cousins.

• Pterosaur hip bone • Dinosaur hip bone

PREHISTORIC TIME

In this book, you'll learn about 30 bizarre flying creatures, from the tiny *Nemicolopterus* to the airplane-sized *Quetzalcoatlus*. All these creatures lived on Earth during different time periods.

TRIASSIC PERIOD

From 252 to 201 million years ago. Pterosaurs and dinosaurs first evolved during this period.

JURASSIC PERIOD

From 201 to 145 million years ago. Also known as the "Age of Giants." Some of the largest dinosaurs lived during this period. It's also when birds, a group of dinosaurs, first evolved.

TRIASSIC   JURASSIC   CRETACEOUS   PALEOC

MESOZOIC ERA

CRETACEOUS PERIOD

From 145 to 66 million years ago. This is when some of the most famous dinosaurs, like the *Triceratops* and *Tyrannosaurus*, lived. At the end of this period, all dinosaurs except birds became **extinct** when an asteroid hit Earth.

CENOZOIC ERA

From 66 million years ago through today. Also known as the "Age of Mammals."

...ENE	OLIGOCENE	MIOCENE	PLIOCENE	PLEISTOCENE	HOLOCENE

CENOZOIC ERA

CAELESTIVENTUS

Other pterosaurs lived in forests or near water, but *Caelestiventus* lived in the desert. It had over 100 pointy teeth that it probably used to eat small animals. Because pterosaur bones are thin and delicate, they often get squished during **fossilization**. *Caelestiventus* is a special fossil because many of its parts were not squished. To study these fragile bones, scientists scanned the rocks at a hospital to examine them on a computer.

Caelestiventus is one of the largest pterosaurs from the Triassic period.

Wingspan: 5 feet

When: Late Triassic—208 million years ago

Where: Western United States

It ate: perhaps insects and small reptiles. Paleontologists don't know.

It was the size of: a cat

JEHOLOPTERUS

SAY IT! ja-hole-OP-tur-us
TYPE: Pterosaur

CAIHONG

SAY IT! Ki-hong
TYPE: Dinosaur

Wingspan: 2.5 feet

When: Middle-Late Jurassic—160 million years ago

Where: China

It ate: insects or fish

It was the size of: a duck

Wingspan: about 3 feet

When: Late Jurassic—161 million years ago

Where: China

It ate: maybe small reptiles or other small, feathered dinosaurs

It was the size of: a duck

Usually, the hard parts of an animal, like bones and teeth, become fossils. *Jeholopterus* is a special fossil that has not only bones but also soft parts, like skin from the wings. The pterosaur *Jeholopterus* lived around the same time as *Caihong*, a small dinosaur with amazing colors! Pigment cells called **melanosomes** in fossils tell us that *Caihong*'s feathers were **iridescent**!

Caihong *likely glided from tree to tree, just like flying squirrels do today.*

YI

SAY IT! Ee / TYPE: Dinosaur

Paleontologists think that Yi was a yellow-brown color.

Yi belonged to one of the weirdest groups of dinosaurs, Scansoriopterygidae (scan-sore-e-OP-tur-RIDGE-ah-day). With a short head and a small, round snout, *Yi* had only a few angled teeth at the front of its mouth. *Yi*'s wings were also unusual. Like a pterosaur, *Yi* had a very long finger that supported much of the skin of the wing. It also had a rod of **cartilage** in the middle of the wing to stiffen it and provide support.

In Chinese, Yi's full scientific name—Yi qi—means "strange wing."

Wingspan: 20 inches

When: Middle and Late Jurassic—160 million years ago

Where: China

It ate: insects

It was the size of: a magpie

TRIASSIC **JURASSIC** CRETACEOUS CENOZOIC

Anchiornis *means* "near bird," because it was an important fossil for learning how small meat-eating dinosaurs evolved to birds.

ANCHIORNIS

SAY IT! ang-key-OR-niss / TYPE: Dinosaur

Fossils of *Anchiornis*, a feathered dinosaur from China, have taught paleontologists many important facts—especially about color. Instead of studying only one feather from the fossil of *Anchiornis*, scientists studied different feathers from all over its body. This taught scientists that *Anchiornis* had many colors on its body, like some modern birds!

Anchiornis **spat out** gastric pellets—*just like owls and other predatory birds do today!*

It *was gray with black- and white-speckled wings and had a bright red crest of feathers on its head.*

Wingspan: about 3 feet

When: Late Jurassic—160 million years ago

Where: China

It ate: lizards and fish

It was the size of: a crow

ARCHAEOPTERYX

SAY IT! r-key-OP-tur-icks / **TYPE:** Dinosaur

Archaeopteryx is perhaps the most famous fossil of all time because it is a **transitional fossil** that proved that birds evolved from dinosaurs. When it was first discovered, scientists were debating the origin of birds. *Archaeopteryx* surprised everyone because it had features of both dinosaurs and birds. It was a small, meat-eating dinosaur with teeth, long arms, claws, a long tail, and feathered wings! Some paleontologists think that *Archaeopteryx* used its claws to climb up trees, then jumped and glided from tree to tree.

Wingspan: 2 feet

When: Late Jurassic—150 to 148 million years ago

Where: Germany

It ate: small reptiles, and maybe even other small dinosaurs

It was the size of: a crow

You can see the most famous Archaeopteryx fossil, known as the "Berlin Specimen," at the Berlin Museum of Natural History in Berlin, Germany.

TRIASSIC | **JURASSIC** | CRETACEOUS | CENOZOIC

PTERODACTYLUS

The famous *Pterodactylus* was the first pterosaur ever found. At first, scientists were not sure what kind of animal it was. Some thought *Pterodactylus* was a sea creature. Others thought it might have been a flying **marsupial**, the group of animals that kangaroos and koalas belong to. When scientists first made drawings to imagine what *Pterodactylus* looked like when it was alive, they modeled their designs after a bat!

Wingspan: just over 3 feet

When: Late Jurassic—150 to 148 million years ago

Where: Germany

It ate: fish and other small animals

It was the size of: a raven

Pterodactylus *lived alongside* **Archaeopteryx.**

French scientist Georges Cuvier originally called it "Ptéro-Dactyle," but scientific names need to be in Latin, so the name was changed from Pterodactyl to Pterodactylus.

CONFUCIUSORNIS

SAY IT! kun-FEW-sush-OR-niss
TYPE: Bird

Wingspan: just over 2 feet

When: Early Cretaceous—
125 to 120 million years ago

Where: China

It ate: fish

It was the size of:
a pigeon

MICRORAPTOR

SAY IT! MY-crow-RAP-tor
TYPE: Dinosaur

Wingspan: 3 feet

When: Early Cretaceous—
120 million years ago

Where: China

It ate: small mammals, birds, lizards, and fish

It was the size of:
a raven

Confuciusornis is the oldest known bird to have a beak like those of modern birds. The male had two tail feathers that were nearly as long as its entire body! The dinosaur *Microraptor* lived alongside *Confuciusornis*. Like other birds, *Microraptor* had one set of wings on its arms, but it also had another pair on its legs. Paleontologists think that *Microraptor* used its four wings to glide from tree to tree.

Confuciusornis *was named in honor of the Chinese philosopher Confucius.*

Tupandactylus had two bones sticking out from its skull. Between them was keratin—the same stuff our fingernails are made of!

TUPANDACTYLUS

SAY IT! two-pan-DAK-tul-us / **TYPE:** Pterosaur

Named after Tupi, a god of thunder, *Tupandactylus* means "Tupi finger," because a pterosaur's wing is made of one long finger bone. Imagine if your ring fingers were longer than your body—that's what a pterosaur's wing was like! *Tupandactylus* had short, deep jaws and a long skull with a "sail," or crest, of **keratin** on top. It lived along the edge of a giant, ancient lake. Some paleontologists believe that *Tupandactylus* used its strange head like a sail to glide and steer above the waves.

Wingspan: 16 feet

When: Early Cretaceous—112 million years ago

Where: Brazil

It ate: fruit and tough seeds, or fish

It was the size of: a car

Paleontologists don't know what Tupandactylus's crest was for. Was it to control their direction when flying or maybe help identify other species? Or was it just for display, similar to a peacock's tail?

ORNITHOCHEIRUS

SAY IT! or-nith-O-ki-russ / **TYPE:** Pterosaur

The name *Ornithocheirus* means "bird hand." When *Ornithocheirus* fossils were first found, paleontologists thought pterosaurs were the direct ancestors of birds. We now know that pterosaurs and birds are not related! Even though both creatures have wings that include the bones of the hand and finger, a pterosaur's wing is very different from a bird's wing. When two animals that are unrelated have a similar shape or design, scientists call it **convergent evolution** (con-VIR-gint).

Instead of a fancy head crest, Ornithocheirus *had a long bill with a rounded tip.*

Wingspan: 16 feet

When: Early Cretaceous—113 to 110 million years ago

Where: United Kingdom

It ate: fish

Its wingspan was the size of: a giraffe

The second part of Ludodactylus's scientific name is sibbicki, *in honor of the famous paleoartist John Sibbick.*

LUDODACTYLUS

Ludodactylus looked a lot like another pterosaur called *Pteranodon*—except it had teeth. In fact, *Ludodactylus* was the first pterosaur found that had both a big head crest and teeth. We have only one fossil of *Ludodactylus*, which has a leaf stuck in its mouth! Paleontologists believe that this *Ludodactylus* saw the leaf floating on the water and mistook it for a fish. The leaf then got stuck in its mouth, making it hard for *Ludodactylus* to catch fish.

The leaf stuck in its mouth was from a yucca plant. Yucca plants are still around today!

Wingspan: 13 feet

When: Early Cretaceous—112 million years ago

Where: Brazil

It ate: fish

It was the size of: a large dolphin

The second part of Thalassodromeus's scientific name is sethi, *in honor of the Egyptian god Seth.*

The giant triangular head crest of Thalassodromeus makes it one of the biggest pterosaur skulls.

THALASSODROMEUS

The name *Thalassodromeus* means "sea runner," because the paleontologists who named it thought that it flew fast above the water, skimming fish. But the shape of *Thalassodromeus*'s bill is very different from the bills of water-skimming birds today. New research suggests that *Thalassodromeus* flew over land and used its big, strong bill to catch smaller land animals. *Thalassodromeus* might have even eaten small dinosaurs!

Some paleontologists think that Thalassodromeus *is not its own species but rather a fully grown pterosaur called* Tupuxuara.

Wingspan: 17 feet

When: Early Cretaceous— 110 million years ago

Where: Brazil

It ate: small animals

Its wingspan was the size of: an adult hippopotamus

PTERODAUSTRO

Pterodaustro had an unusual bill with long jaws that were curved and filled with bristle-like teeth. There's a flying animal today that also has curved, bristle-filled jaws—flamingos! Because their jaws are so similar, paleontologists think that *Pterodaustro* sifted through the water for food just like a flamingo does. From studying the eyes of *Pterodaustro* paleontologists found that this creature was most active in the evenings, just like many geese, ducks, and swans are today.

Wingspan: 4.5 feet

When: Early Cretaceous—105 million years ago

Where: Argentina

It ate: small animals

Its wingspan was the size of: an average 10-year-old

Pterodaustro *was one of the first pterosaurs discovered in South America.*

Flamingos are pink because of the colors in the tiny shrimp and algae they eat, so Pterodaustro might have been pink as well.

TRIASSIC | JURASSIC | CRETACEOUS | CENOZOIC

Paleontologists found a fossil of a Pterodaustro egg with an embryo inside it.

Nemicolopterus lived in lush inland forests filled with many different kinds of pterosaurs and dinosaurs.

NEMICOLOPTERUS

Nemicolopterus lived in the thick forests of ancient China. We often think that all prehistoric creatures were gigantic, but that's not true! Many were tiny, and *Nemicolopterus* was likely the smallest pterosaur. The body of *Nemicolopterus* was only about 2 inches long.

Wingspan: 10 inches

When: Early Cretaceous—120 million years ago

Where: China

It ate: insects and fruit

It was the size of: a robin

Paleontologists don't know if Nemicolopterus *is the smallest pterosaur or just a baby of another pterosaur.*

Many other forest-dwelling pterosaurs had teeth for catching insects and small reptiles, but *Nemicolopterus* didn't. So, what did it eat? Perhaps small insects that it didn't need teeth to catch. Or maybe it ate fruit or leaves.

HESPERORNIS

SAY IT! hess-purr-OR-niss / TYPE: Bird

Imagine a cross between a penguin and a duck. Now give it teeth. That's probably what *Hesperornis* looked like. Like penguins, *Hesperornis* was flightless and swam in the ocean to catch fish. But instead of flapping their wings to swim, *Hesperornis* moved through the water with its large, paddle-like feet like a duck or loon. Unlike penguins, which live in cold climates, *Hesperornis* lived in warm tropical areas similar to the Southeastern United States.

Hesperornis was found by the famous paleontologist Othniel Charles Marsh.

Wingspan: unknown

When: Early Cretaceous— 83 to 78 million years ago

Where: North America

It ate: fish

It was the size of: an adult human

In movies, Pteranodon *is shown picking up things with its feet like an eagle, but its feet were too small and weak to do this.*

PTERANODON

We know more about *Pteranodon* than any other pterosaur because we have hundreds of fossils of this large flying creature. With its long, thin bill and sickle-shaped crest, *Pteranodon* lived at the edge of an ancient ocean in the middle of North America. A female *Pteranodon* was about half the size of a male. Only the males had a giant crest on the back of their heads, just like male deer have antlers but females don't. The crest of male *Pteranodon* may have been used to attract a mate.

Pteranodon fossils have been found with digested fish inside.

Wingspan: 22 feet

When: Late Cretaceous—86 to 84 million years ago

Where: North America

It ate: fish

Its wingspan was the size of: a two-story building

NYCTOSAURUS

Nyctosaurus has one of the coolest head crests of all pterosaurs, a forked crest that was twice as long as its body! Its crest changed and grew longer as it became an adult. Paleontologists used to think that there was skin between the bone crest—just like the sail on a sailboat. However, studying how crests functioned in flight, paleontologists determined that a skin-sail on the crest would not help *Nyctosaurus*.

All other pterosaurs had clawed fingers on their wings—but not Nyctosaurus!

It was discovered by the famous paleontologist Othniel Charles Marsh, who also discovered Pteranodon.

Wingspan: 6 feet

When: Late Cretaceous—85 to 84 million years ago

Where: United States

It ate: fish

Its wingspan was the size of: an average adult

Nyctosaurus
*lived with the
famous pterosaur*
Pteranodon.

Once in the air, Quetzalcoatlus may have kept its wings stretched out and glided like a giant kite.

Not only was the wingspan of Quetzalcoatlus huge, the creature was also very tall when walking on land. A standing Quetzalcoatlus was as tall as a giraffe!

QUETZALCOATLUS

Soaring above the ancient plains of western North America, the giant *Quetzalcoatlus* might be the largest flying animal that ever lived on Earth! *Quetzalcoatlus* is named after the legendary god Quetzalcoatl (pronounced ket-za-co-OT-ull). Paleontologists aren't sure what it ate. Some think it was like a vulture and fed on dead dinosaurs. Some think it grabbed fish when flying low to the water. Others think it walked around and snatched up small animals—like baby dinosaurs.

The United States military used a model of Quetzalcoatlus *to design an experimental airplane.*

Wingspan: 40 feet

When: Late Cretaceous—68 to 66 million years ago

Where: Western United States

It ate: dead dinosaurs, fish, or small animals

It was the size of: a small airplane

Hatzegopteryx *lived on an island with no large meat-eating dinosaurs. It probably evolved to fill the important role of a predator in the ecosystem.*

HATZEGOPTERYX

Hatzegopteryx lived at the same time as *Quetzalcoatlus*, and both are among the largest animals that have ever flown. Though the wingspan of *Quetzalcoatlus* is a little longer, *Hatzegopteryx*'s bones are much bigger. Unlike other giant pterosaurs, *Hatzegopteryx* has a short neck. It probably chased its prey, but what did it eat? Paleontologists think it ate dwarf dinosaurs, which lived on the same island where *Hatzegopteryx* lived. One of these dwarf dinosaurs was a **sauropod** called *Magyarosaurus* (maeg-yar-o-SORE-us), a long-necked, plant-eating dinosaur about the size of a cow.

Wingspan: 38 feet

When: Late Cretaceous—66 million years ago

Where: Romania

It ate: dwarf dinosaurs

It was the size of: a giraffe

The island Hatzegopteryx lived on was covered in thick forests of beech, birch, and walnut trees—all trees that are still around today!

ONYCHONYCTERIS

Onychonycteris is the oldest bat fossil! Along with pterosaurs and birds, bats make up the third group of flying **vertebrates**, or animals with backbones. *Onychonycteris* looks like a normal bat, but it's also different in many ways. By observing the tiny bones inside its ears, paleontologists found that *Onychonycteris* could not **echolocate**, which is how modern bats "see" by using sound. Since *Onychonycteris* appeared on Earth only 14 million years after the dinosaurs went extinct, some of the earliest bats may have lived with dinosaurs.

Wingspan: 12 inches

When: Early Eocene— 52 million years ago

Where: Western United States

It ate: fruit or insects

It was the size of: a cardinal

Modern bats have toes that are all the same length. Onychonycteris's toes were all different lengths, indicating it did not hang upside-down like bats do today.

ANTHROPORNIS

Anthropornis was one of the biggest penguins that has ever lived! But *Anthropornis* was not exactly like the penguins you know. It had wings that were somewhat flexible, not rigid like the flippers of modern penguins. One extinct penguin, *Inkayacu* (ink-ah-YAH-coo), was reddish-brown and black—not black-and-white like penguins today!

Wingspan: unknown

When: Eocene and Oligocene Epochs—45 to 33 million years ago

Where: Antarctica

It ate: fish

It was the size of: an adult human

Anthropornis means "human bird," so named because it was as big as a person.

It was almost two feet taller than today's largest penguin, the Emperor Penguin.

Eurotrochilus was likely brightly colored and iridescent, like hummingbirds today.

Its beak was about 2.5 times longer than the rest of its skull.

EUROTROCHILUS

Unlike many of the birds in this book, *Eurotrochilus* was tiny. With a body just over 1 inch long, *Eurotrochilus* zipped around in search of flowers. *Eurotrochilus* is the earliest known ancestor of hummingbirds!

Today, hummingbirds live in North and South America. But *Eurotrochilus* is extra special because it lived in Europe. How did a prehistoric hummingbird fly to the other side of the planet? Paleontologists don't know, but it's one more thing that makes hummingbirds such amazing and fascinating birds.

All hummingbirds have specially shaped wing bones that allow them to fly forward, backward, sideways, and hover in place—they are the only birds that can do this!

Wingspan: under 2 inches

When: Early Oligocene Epoch—34 to 28 million years ago

Where: France, Germany, and Poland

It ate: flower nectar

It was the size of: a small mouse

DROMORNIS

SAY IT! dro-MORE-niss / TYPE: Bird

Dromornis belongs to an amazing group of giant, extinct, flightless birds from Australia, commonly called the mihirungs (MEE-hee-rungs). These giant-beaked birds were closely related to ducks and geese or chickens and turkeys. *Dromornis* had big, bulky feet and powerful legs. But these legs were not built for running. *Dromornis* probably plodded along and walked everywhere. *Dromornis*'s huge beak looks scary, but it was used to crush plant roots, big seeds, and nuts.

Paleontologists used to think the mihirungs were just giant, flightless geese.

Height: almost 10 feet

Weight: 1,600 pounds

When: Late Miocene and Early Pliocene Epochs— 28 to 5 million years ago

Where: Australia

It ate: plants, seeds, and nuts

It was the size of: a cow

Dromornis was named in 1872 by the most famous anatomist of all time—Richard Owen.

At first, paleontologists were confused by Dromornis's big beak and thought that it ate meat.

Like modern sea birds, Pelagornis *had a large salt gland in its eye sockets. This gland helps store and get rid of extra salt from ocean water.*

PELAGORNIS

Pelagornis was a giant sea bird and might have been the largest flying bird ever. Even though *Pelagornis* looked like a giant albatross, it was more closely related to pelicans and storks. You might think its long beak is filled with dozens of sharp pointy "teeth," but they are not teeth! Those "fake teeth" are actually growths from the bones that make the beak. These helped *Pelagornis* catch and hold on to slippery fish.

Wingspan: about 20 feet

When: Late Oligocene and Early Pleistocene Epochs— 25 to 2 million years ago

Where: United States, Chile, France, Morocco, and New Zealand

It ate: fish

Its wingspan was the size of: a giraffe

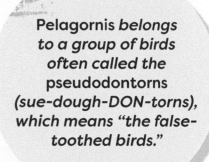

Pelagornis *belongs to a group of birds often called the* pseudodontorns *(sue-dough-DON-torns), which means "the false-toothed birds."*

HERACLES

Heracles was the largest parrot of all time! The heaviest parrot alive today, the kakapo (KACK-ah-poh), weighs nine pounds and reaches the knee of an adult. But *Heracles* would have reached an adult's waist and it weighed over 15 pounds! Paleontologists have found only two leg bones from *Heracles*, so they do not know much about this bird. But by comparing those leg bones to modern parrot bones, paleontologists can make scientific guesses about size, shape, diet, and behavior of *Heracles*.

Wingspan: unknown

When: Early Miocene—19 to 16 million years ago

Where: New Zealand

It ate: berries, fruit, and nuts

It was the size of: a Great Dane (a breed of large dog)

Because of its large size, paleontologists think that Heracles was flightless, just like the kakapo.

KELENKEN

SAY IT! kell-IN-kin
TYPE: Bird

Wingspan: unknown

When: Middle Miocene—
15 million years ago

Where: Argentina

It ate: large rodents, snakes, and deer-like animals

It was as tall as:
an elephant

ARGENTAVIS

SAY IT! r-gin-TAY-vuss
TYPE: Bird

Wingspan: 21 feet

When: Late Miocene—
9 to 6 million years ago

Where: Argentina

It ate: dead animals

It was the size of:
a killer whale

Standing over 10 feet tall, *Kelenken* was a top predator with a large, powerful beak. But *Kelenken* didn't fly to catch unsuspecting prey—it ran after its prey. While *Kelenken* ran on the ground, the giant *Argentavis* soared in the skies above. Riding on air currents like modern condors and vultures, *Argentavis* likely patrolled the skies for prey. Its large beak and claws could have been used for catching prey, but paleontologists think that *Argentavis* probably fed on already dead animals.

VOROMBE

Vorombe belongs to a group of big, flightless birds called "elephant birds." Almost 10 feet tall, *Vorombe* was estimated to weigh 1,900 pounds, making it the heaviest bird of all time! It had tiny wings and walked around on powerful legs. Paleontologists think that it had a good sense of smell and was active at night. You might think that elephant birds were related to today's ostriches or emus, but they're not! Their closest relative is the small, flightless, **nocturnal** kiwi from New Zealand.

Wingspan: unknown

When: Pleistocene and Holocene Epochs—2 million to 1,000 years ago

Where: Madagascar

It ate: fruit, seeds, and nuts

It was as tall as: a basketball hoop

Elephant birds laid the largest egg of all time—it could hold about 150 chicken eggs!

HIERAAETUS

Hieraaetus, also known as the Haast's eagle, is the largest eagle that ever lived. With a wingspan of nearly 10 feet and weighing over 30 pounds, *Hieraaetus* soared above the forests and grasslands of New Zealand. *Hieraaetus* had claws that were 3 inches long. It was the top predator in its ecosystem and preyed on the moa (MO-ah), which were large, flightless birds similar to the elephant birds. Several moa fossils show broken bones caused by *Hieraaetus*'s talons and beak.

Wingspan: almost 10 feet

When: Pleistocene and Holocene Epochs— 2.5 million to 500 years ago

Where: New Zealand

It ate: meat

It was the size of: a golden eagle, but much heavier

Hieraaetus *lived on Earth so recently that the native people of New Zealand, the Māori, have folktales about living alongside it.*

Glossary

anatomist: A scientist who studies the structure of bodies.

cartilage: Tissue that makes up your nose and ears. Cartilage is softer and more flexible than keratin or bone, but still provides support and shape for body parts.

convergent evolution: When plants or animals look similar but are not related. For example, a shark and a dolphin are similarly shaped because they both swim in the ocean, not because they are closely related.

crest: A tuft of feathers, bone, or skin on the head of an animal.

echolocate: "Seeing" with sound. Animals like bats, whales, and dolphins make high-pitched sounds that create a picture of what's around them.

evolution: All plants and animals change over time. Through multiple generations, small changes add up and cause a new species to be different from the old one.

extinct: Having died out and completely disappeared, as with plants and animals that used to live on Earth.

fossils: The remains of plants and animals that have slowly been turned to stone by minerals in the ground.

fossilization: The process of turning a plant or animal into stone.

gastric pellets: Parts of a bird's food that they spit out rather than digest.

iridescent: Shiny and appearing like different colors from different angles. The color of a soap bubble is an example of iridescence.

keratin: A type of protein that makes up hair and fingernails. Keratin can be very hard, but it's not bone.

marsupial: Order of mammals that include kangaroos, koalas, and possums.

melanosomes: Part of a cell that stores color. The size, shape, and order of melanosomes in an animal's cell can determine what color its skin or feathers are.

nocturnal: Awake and active at night. Owls are nocturnal animals.

paleontologists: Scientists who study fossils to learn about the plants and animals that used to live on Earth.

prehistoric: The time before humans and written history.

pterosaurs: Flying reptiles that lived at the same time as the dinosaurs. They were not dinosaurs, but close evolutionary relatives.

pycnofibers: Hair-like fibers on pterosaurs. Pycnofibers are not hair, but they are very similar and probably helped keep pterosaurs warm, just like hair helps keep mammals warm.

sauropod: The largest land animal that ever lived. Sauropods are dinosaurs with long necks and tails. They stood on four legs and ate only plants.

transitional fossil: A fossil that has traits common to both creatures that lived before it and creatures that lived after it.

vertebrate: Any animal with a skeleton made up of bones or cartilage.

wingspan: The distance that a creature's wings stretch, from tip to tip.

Index

O

Onychonycteris, 42–43

Ornithocheirus, 22–23

Owen, Richard, 49

P

Paleontologists, 2

Pelagornis, 50–51

Penguins, 44–45

Pseudodontorns, 51

Pteranodon, 34–35

Pterodactylus, 16–17

Pterodaustro, 28–29

Pterosaurs, 2–3

Q

Quetzalcoatlus, 38–39

R

Russel, Alfred, 15

S

Sauropods, 41

Scansoriopterygidae, 10

T

Thalassodromeus, 26–27

Transitional fossils, 14

Triassic Period, 4

Tupandactylus, 20–21

V

Vertebrates, 42

Vorombe, 56–57

Y

Yi, 10–11

About the Author

Cary Woodruff grew up in rural central Virginia and received his bachelor's and master's degrees at Montana State University under famed dinosaur paleontologist Dr. Jack Horner. Currently, Cary is the Director of Paleontology at the Great Plains Dinosaur Museum in Malta, Montana. Cary is also a doctoral student at the University of Toronto under Dr. David Evans. Cary specializes in sauropod dinosaurs. His pioneering studies on sauropod growth are changing our understanding of the lives of the biggest animals to ever walk on Earth. Cary has also published research on the first burrowing dinosaur, modern cow vertebral anatomy, dinosaur vision, stegosaurs, and fossil manatees in ancient Egyptian catacombs.

About the Illustrators

Annalisa and Marina Durante are nature and science illustrators. They are twin sisters who have loved nature and animals since they were children. Marina enjoys hiking, deep-water diving, and photography. The photos she takes while exploring nature are the inspiration for her art. Annalisa is inspired by Eastern philosophy and enjoys meditating as she explores the outdoors.

In 2001, Marina and Annalisa were invited by the Galapagos National Park to draw the birds of the Galapagos Islands. They have worked for the Food and Agriculture Organization (FAO) of the United Nations, illustrating recently discovered species of fish. Their works have been published all over the world, and they have won a number of international art prizes. They especially enjoy illustrating portraits of animals and pets. Find them online at www.duranteillustrations.com.

CPSIA information can be obtained
at www.ICGtesting.com
Printed in the USA
JSHW041622020620
6040JS00006B/154